FLOWERS OF ORNAMENTAL GARDEN PLANTS

42 pages

185 Coloured Illustrations
with
Botanical Names

Robert W Strugnell

Published by Robert W Strugnell
www.fitzroygardens.com

First Published 2016

ISBN 978-0-9954330-4-5

CONTENTS

1. Clematis caerulea.   2. Clematis sieboldii.   3. Illicium floridanum.

1. Anemone japonica.   2. Anemone capensis.   3. Anemone palmata.

1. Cistus purpureus.   2. Cistus vaginatus.   3. Cistus formosus.
4. Cistus algarvensis.   5. Cistus incanus.

1. Polygala speciosa.   2. Polygala chamaebuxus.   3. Polygala bracteolata.
4. Muraltia mixta.

1. Malva umbellata.   2. Malva creeana.
3. Linum arboreum.   4. Linum trigynum.

1. Hibiscus militaris.   2. Hibiscus cameroni fulgens.
3. Hibiscus lilacinus.   4. Hibiscus manihot.

1. Abutilon striatum.   2. Abutilon vitifolium. 3. Abutilon graveolens.

1. Sollya heterophylla.   2. Billardiera mutabilis. 3. Pittosporum tobira.

1. Marianthus coeruleo-punctatus. 2. Pronaya elegans.
3. Tetratheca hirsuta.   4. Tetratheca verticillata.

9

1. Sarracenia purpurea.   2. Sarracenia flava.   3. Capparis acuminata.

1. Reevesia thyrsoidea.   2. Lasiopetalum quercifolium.
3. Hermannia flammea.   4. Mahernia grandiflora.

1. Camellia japonica.   2. Camellia japonica chandleri.
3. Camellia japonica pomponia.   4. Camellia japonica anemoneflora.

1. Camellia reticulata.   2. Camellia oleifera.
3. Camellia maliflora.   4. Thea viridis.

1. Hypericum monogynum.   2. Hypericum uralum.
3. Hypericum balearicum.   4. Reaumuria hypericoides.

1. Geranium anemonefolium. 2. Pelargonium tricolor.
3. Pelargonium crassicaule. 4. Pelargonium peltatum. 5. Pelargonium zonale.

1. Pelargonium Large-flowered White. 2. Pelargonium Gem.
3. Pelargonium Sunrise. 4. Pelargonium Anais.

1. Tropaeolum azureum.   2. Tropaeolum polyphyllum.
3. Tropaeolum lobbianum.   4. Tropaeolum crenatiflorum.

1. Diosma speciosa.   2. Diosma fragrans.
3. Diosma pulchella.   4. Diosma hirta.

1. Boronia serrulata.   2. Boronia crenulata.
3. Crowea saligna.   4. Eriostemon buxifolium.

1. Corraea alba.   2. Corraea pulchella.
3. Corraea speciosa.   4. Corraea longiflora.

1. Sophora velutina.   2. Edwardsia microphylla.
3. Cyclopia genistoides.   4. Podalyria buxifolia.

1. Chorozema dicksonii.　　2. Chorozema ovaturn.
3. Chorozema henchmanni.　4. Chorozema varium.　5. Chorozema spartioides.

1. Oxylobium retusum. 2. Brachysema latifolium.   3. Euchilus obcordatus.
4. Dillwynia parvifolia.   5. Eutaxia pungens.   6. Hovea pungens.

23

1. Lalage ornata.   2. Scottia dentata.
3. Templetonia retusa.   4. Crotalaria purpurea.   5. Aspalathus chenopoda.

1. Indigofera violacea.   2. Swainsonia coronillaefolia.   3. Clianthus puniceus.
4. Adesmia loudonia.   5. Kennedya coccinea.   6. Physolobium carinatum.

1. Acacia dentifera.   2. Acacia biflora.
3. Acacia longifolia.   4. Acacia lambertiana.

1. Fuchsia macrantha.   2. Fuchsia serratifolia.
3. Fuchsia splendens.   4. Fuchsia radicans.

1. Cuphea cordata.   2. Cuphea platycentra.
3. Cuphea melvilla.   4. Lagerstroemia indica.

1. Verticordia insignis.   2. Calythrix virgata.
3. Melaleuca neriifolia.   4. Melaleuca squamea.   5. Myrtus communis.

1. Callistemon microstachyum.

2. Angophora cordifolia.   3. Metrosideros speciosa.

1. Passiflora caerulea.
2. Passiflora alato-caerulea.   3. Tacsonia pinnatistipula.

1. Crassula centauroides.

2. Kalosanthes coccinea.   3. Kalosanthes versicolor.

Mesembryanthemum albidum. Mesembryanthemum tricolor.
Mesembryanthemum rubrocinctum. Mesembryanthemum inclaudens.
Mesembryanthemum micans.

1. Escallonia organensis.
2. Hydrangea japonica var. caerulea.   3. Lucnlia gratissima.

1. Bouvardia triphylla.   2. Bouvardia versicolor.
3. Burchellia capensis.   4. Gardenia radicans.

1. Cineraria lanata.   2. Cineraria cruenta.   3. Cineraria populifolia var.
4. Astelma eximium.   5. Triptilion spinosum. 6. Brachycome iberidifolia.
    7. Helichrysum sesamoides.

1. Siphocampylos cavanillesii. 2. Leschenaultia biloba.
3. Leschenaultia formosa. 4. Stylidium graminifolium.
5. Euthales macrophylla.

1. Erica tumida.   2. Erica jacksonii.   3. Erica neillii.
4. Erica aitoniana.   5. Erica banksiana.
6. Erica ardens.   7. Epacris impressa.   8. Styphelia tubiflora.

1. Chironia decussata.   2. Lisianthus russellianus.
3. Tecoma jasminoides.   4. Bignonia telfairiae.   5. Tweedia caerulea.

1. Torenia asiatica.   2. Buddlea lindleyana.   3. Anthocercis viscosa.
4. Rhodochiton volubile.   5. Solanum lycioides.
6. Cestrum aurantiacum.   7. Chaenostoma polyanthum

1. Calceolaria crenatiflora.   2. Calceolaria arachnoidea.
3. Achimenes longiflora.   4. Achimenes patens.   5. Amphicome arguta.

1. Ruellia ciliatiflora.   2. Cyclamen persicum.
3. Primula sinensis.   4. Plumbago capensis.   5. Grevillea punicea.
6. Gnidia oppositifolia. 7. Pimelea incana.

www.ingramcontent.com/pod-product-compliance
Lightning Source LLC
LaVergne TN
LVHW072120070426
835511LV00002B/32